BONGO HAS MANY FRIENDS

Words by

Sandy Loose-Schrantz

Paintings by

Peter Loose

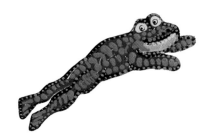

FLYING DOG PRODUCTIONS

Hull, Georgia • Gaithersburg, Maryland

For Lida

FLYING DOG Productions

Flying Dog Productions and the portrayal of Bongo The Flying Dog are trademarks of Flying Dog Productions.

ISBN 0-9660244-1-9

Library of Congress Number LC00-134383

First Edition 2001

Design & Layout by Cindy Jerrell

THANK YOU NINI

**Bongo has many friends.
They are all different
colors and kinds.**

Bongo is friends with **1 black** pig.

Her name is Honey.

**Bongo watches birds
at the feeder.
He spies 2 blue jays**

and **3 red** cardinals.

4 brown dogs are friends with Bongo.

Two are big and
two are little.

Bongo plays hide and seek
with 5 gray squirrels.

When he sees them,
he barks.

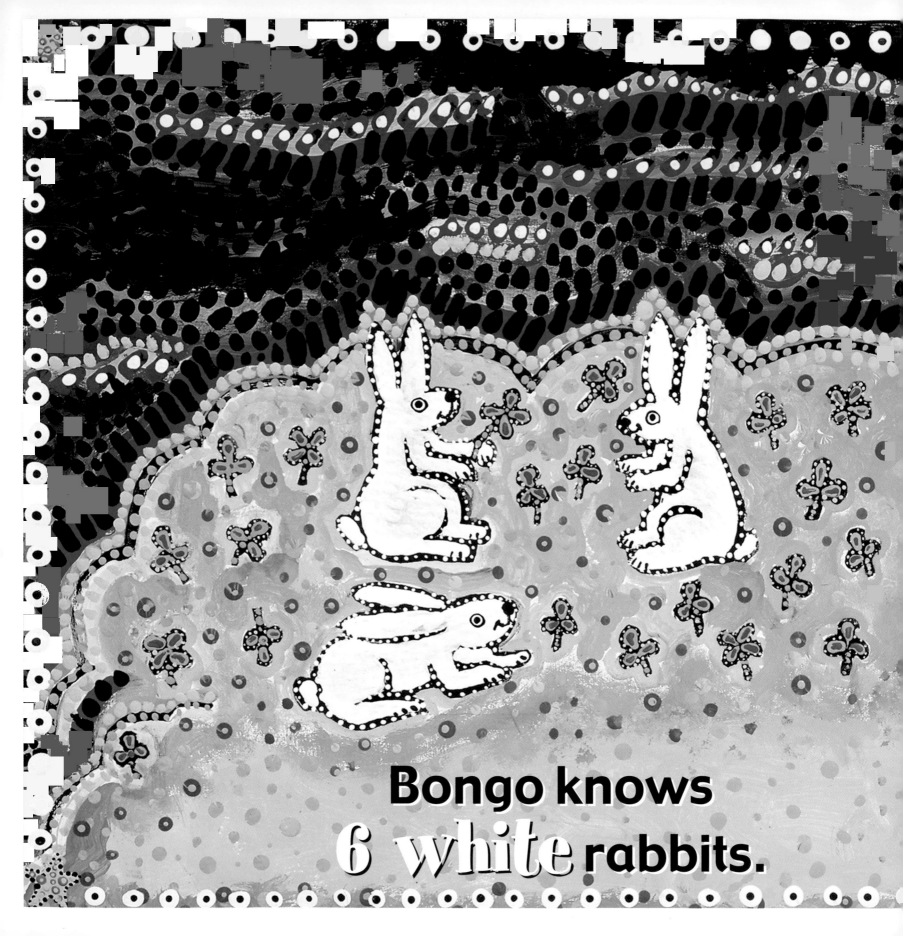

Bongo knows
6 white rabbits.

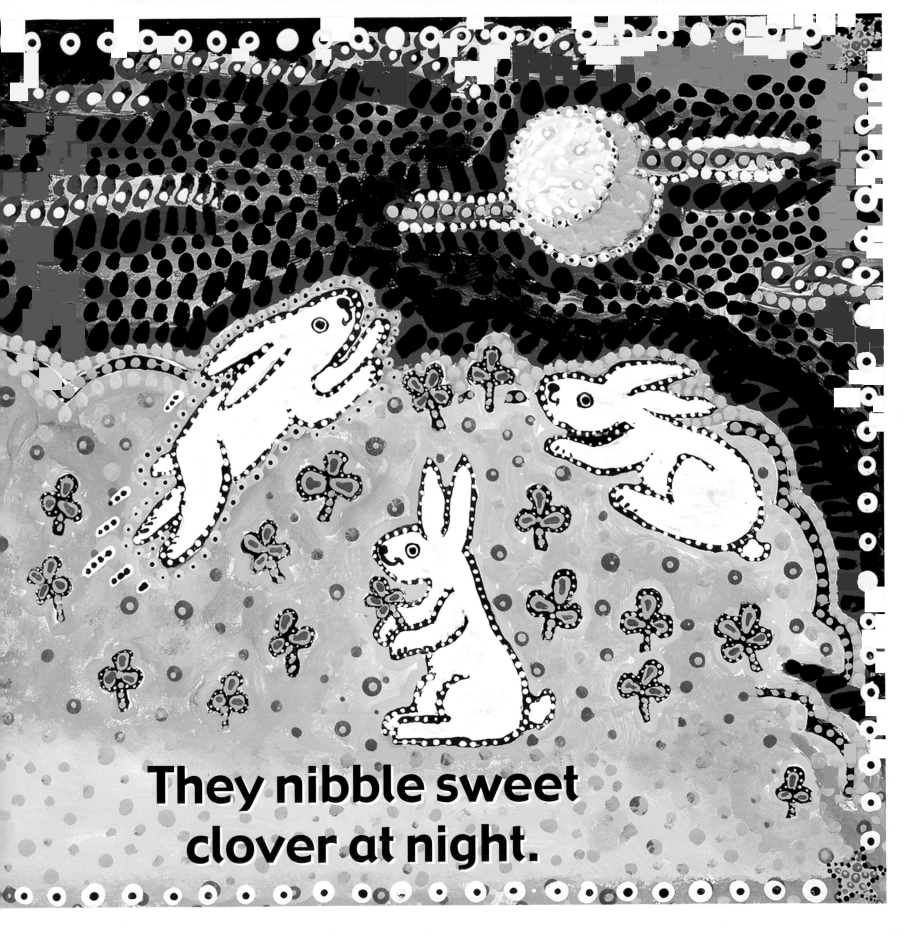

They nibble sweet
clover at night.

7 yellow chicks live in Bongo's yard. Momma Hen keeps them close.

Bongo sees
8 purple butterflies.

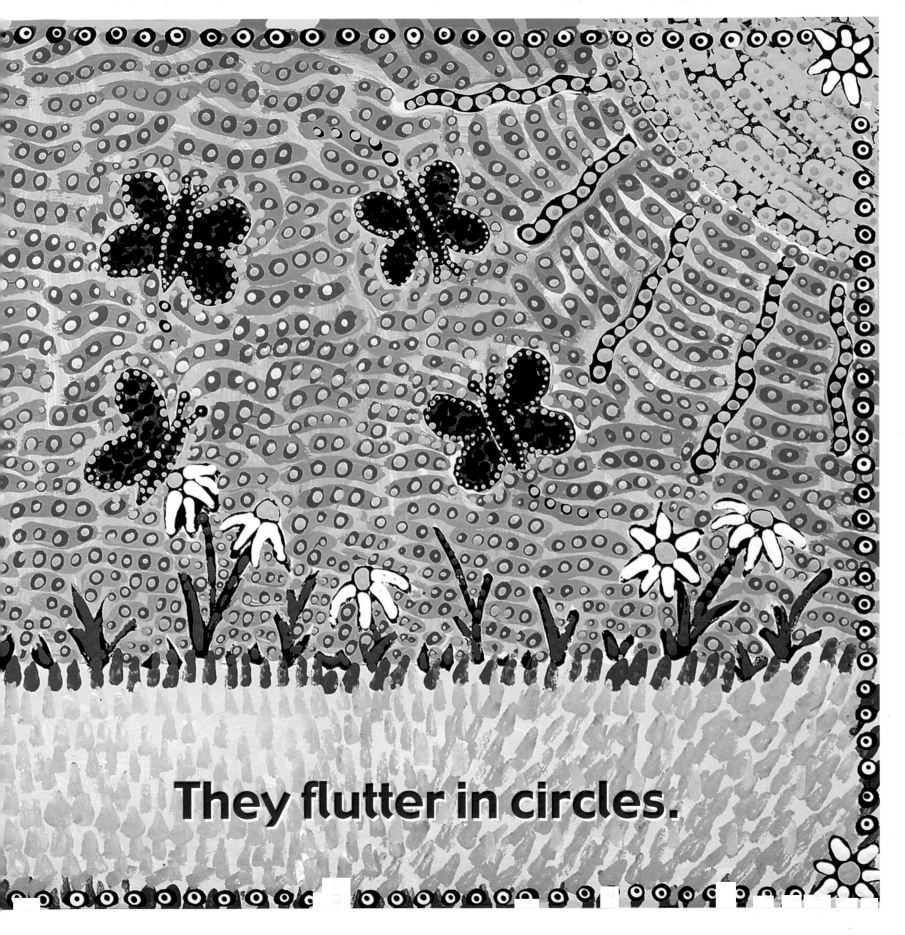

They flutter in circles.

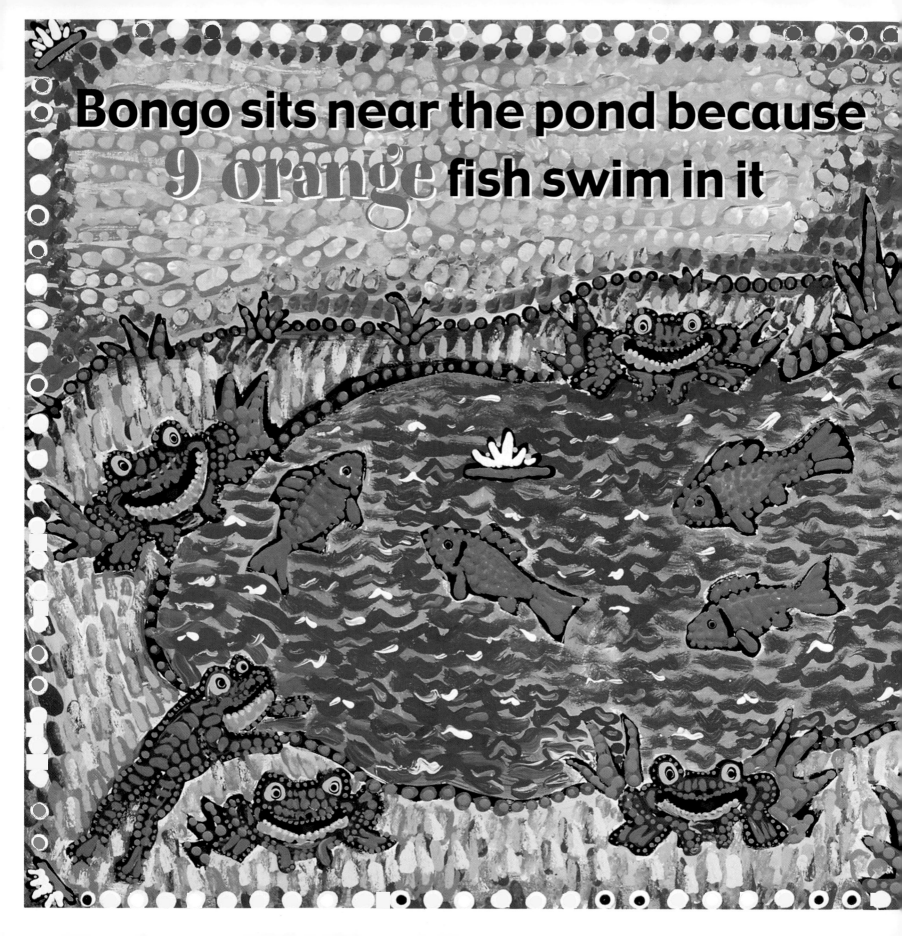

Bongo sits near the pond because 9 orange fish swim in it

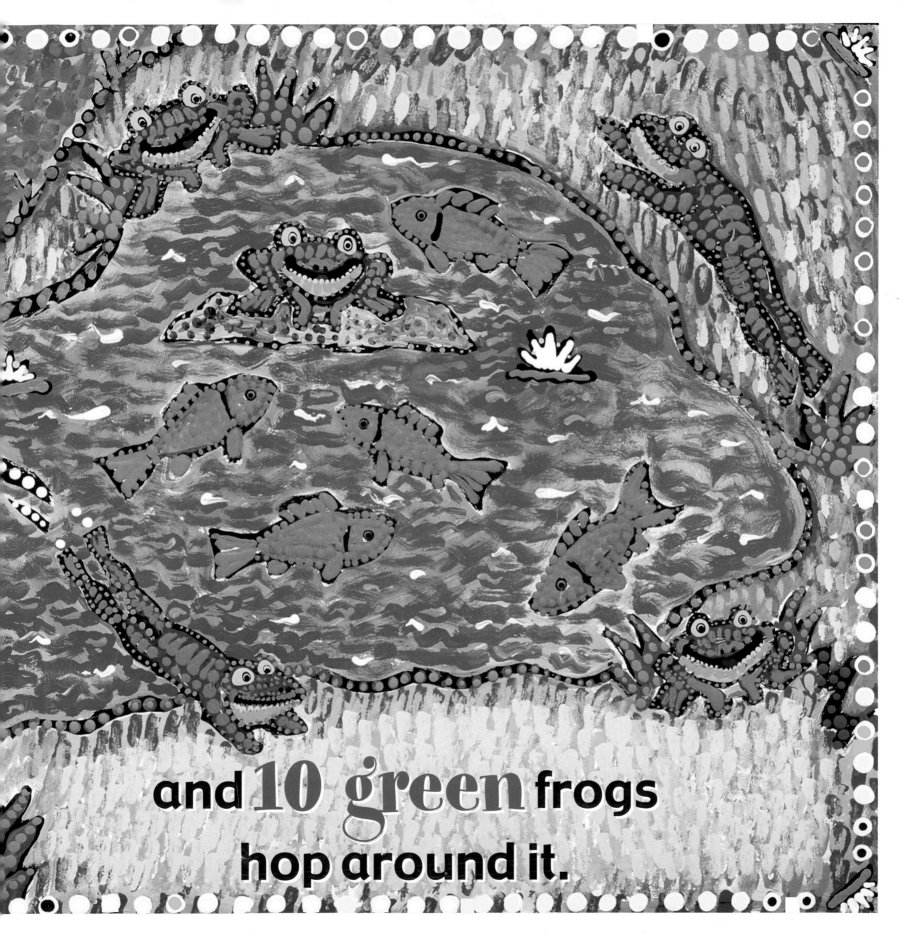

and 10 green frogs
hop around it.

Bongo does have
many friends.

1
2
3
4
5

LOUIE

WOLFIE

P-NUT

LIDA

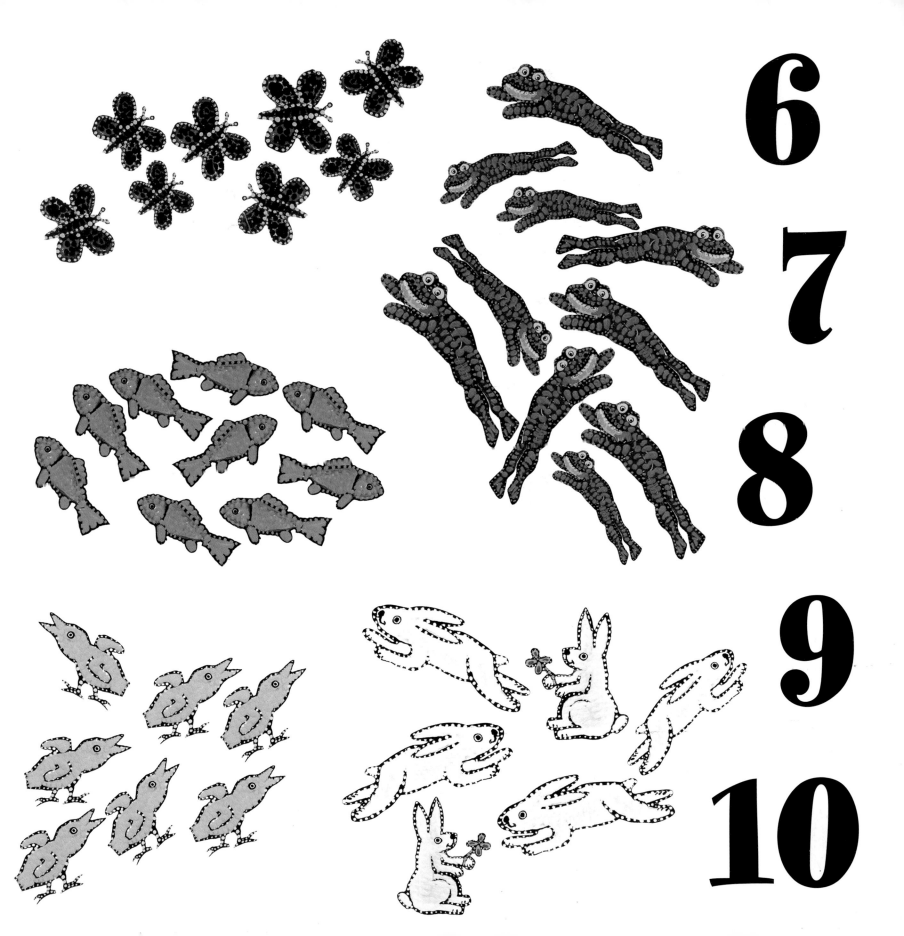

6

7

8

9

10

Here I am with my two best friends, **Pete** and **Sandy**. We live in the country with lots of animals. So just in case you were wondering, <u>Bongo Has Many Friends</u> *is* a true story. Besides the animals you met in the book, we have a goat, an iguana, a snake, and two tarantulas. Many of our critters were adopted from shelters or found on a roadside like me.

Wild animals that live around our place are friends too. Every day squirrels come to eat chicken feed (even though the hens fuss at them). Rabbits visit Pete down by his shop after dark, and once Sandy counted eight hummingbirds buzzing her porch flowers.

We feel so happy living with all these critters. I think when we count animal friends, we are counting our blessings.